U0142047

A NIGHT ON THE PLANE

Yu Hsien

機上的一夜

雨弦中英對照詩集

Foreword I

I was delighted to have been asked by my friend Chung-jinn to contribute to the foreword of his new collection of poems, now accompanied by an English translation. Very shortly after arrival in Taiwan, I had the pleasure of calling on the Director General of the Kaohsiung Broadcasting Station. Chung-Jinn's calm, knowledgeable and reflective perspective on life deeply impressed me. Reading his recent collection of poetry stretching back over several years has been a great pleasure. No poet is ever completely content, but there is a roundness and completion in some of the verse which is very appealing. It is so well crafted that it seems deceptively simple. Yet like good wine it deserves to be taken slowly, sip by sip. I congratulate Chung-jinn on his achievement and hope we shall see more of his work in the future.

David

David Coates
Director General
British Trade And Cultural Office
25 September 2000

Foreword II

I am honored to have been asked by my friend Yu Hsien to write a foreword for the English edition of his poetry collection, A Night on the Plane. I met Yu Hsien soon after my arrival in Kaohsiung and was presented with the Chinese edition of this work. It's a tribute to the clarity of the language that despite my imperfect command of Chinese, I was able to appreciate the work. Like examining one's reflection in a pool of still water, reading Yu Hsien's poems are a door to the examined life. His calm and level gaze on matters of life, love and death encourage contemplation and understanding. I commend them to all lovers of poetry.

Stephen D. Dunn
Branch Chief
Kaohsiung Branch Office
American Institute in Taiwan
Kaohsiung December 28, 2000

自 序

我十六歲開始寫詩，迄今三十餘載，但並非每年都有作品，十九歲到三十一歲期間，只二十四歲有詩四首。儘管如此，詩齡應不算短，作品也逾二百首，除一些被譯成外文，自己從不敢輕言英譯，一來考量自己的英文能力，二來譯詩不比創作，可以迴避，可以爲所欲爲，而是必須去面對，去忠於原作。

一九八五年我首度參加世界詩人大會，日後也有過幾次國際詩會，深感譯詩的重要；近年國際文化交流日頻，文學翻譯愈感迫切需要。去年下半年，我有機會旁聽余光中講授英詩，詩人講詩，語調不疾不徐，內容旁及歷史、地理，善用妙喻，幽默風趣，聽來如沐春風，如入英倫。我一向喜歡英文，英譯的興緻終被點燃。

因此，在去年下半年，我果眞譯起自己的詩作來，五十二首短詩（靈魂之死一首除外），整整花了半年時間。有時靈感一來，很快即成就一首，不禁沾沾自喜，但有時「一把心酸淚」，譯了老半天，卻換來「滿紙荒唐言」，只好從頭來過，或者乾脆放棄。我想，譯詩有時眞比寫詩還難哩！

本書是我第一本中英對照自譯選集，作品多爲幾本詩集中選出，並以詩集爲卷名，分爲「夫妻樹」、「母親的手」、「影子」、「籠中無鳥」、「蘋果之傷」及童詩六卷。最早的一首是一九七四年的「水中月」，最晚的一首是一九九八年的童詩「音樂枕頭」，前後跨越二十五年。翻譯的工作雖在半年內完成，但我的態度絕對是嚴謹的。

最後，我要感謝英國貿易文化辦事處處長David Coates、美國在台協會高雄分處處長Stephen D. Dunn賜序；妻秀燕的愛與縱容，給了我自由的創作空間；以及財團法人高雄市文化基金會的贊助出版，謝謝大家。

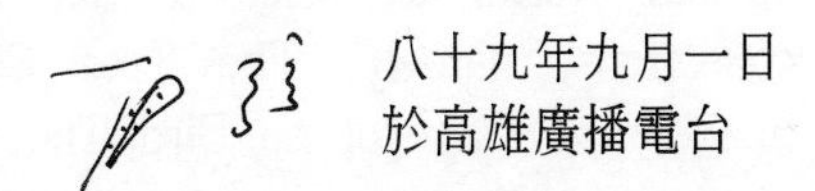

八十九年九月一日
於高雄廣播電台

Preface

I have been writing poems since I was sixteen, for over thirty years now. Not every year did I produce: between the age of 19 and 31, I only wrote four poems at age 24. Nevertheless, it was not a short time overall; my work totaled over two hundred pieces. Several were translated into English. I myself however never dared making an attempt at translating, considering my own English abilities as well as the fact that, while I can be free to express when I write, I have to be truthful to the original when I translate.

Having first attended the World Conference of Poets in 1985 and several international poet conferences thereafter, I have appreciated the importance of poem translation. Translating literature has become increasingly important as international cultural exchange activities expand in recent years. Late last year I had the chance of auditing Professor Kwang-chung Yu's lecture on English poetry. His discussion spanned across history and geography and was full of inspiring and humorous metaphors. Ultimately the lecture sparkled my interest in English translation.

I began translating my own poems. It took me a full six months to translate fifty-two short poems (with the exception of the poem the Death of Souls). When inspiration came, I could quickly translate a poem and would be quite happy with myself; when I put forth great efforts and only created pages of junk, I had to either start over or simply surrender. Translating a poem sometimes was indeed tougher than writing one!

This is my first collection published with English translations. The various works are selected from and titled after several poem collections, namely, The Tree Couple, Mother's Hands, The Shadow, A Cage of no Bird The Wound of an Apple, and six volumes of children's poems. These works spanned over 25 years, from the earliest poem The Moon in Water in 1974 to the children's poem The Music Pillow in 1998. Although the translation was completed within only half a year, I approached it with great care.

I would like to thank David Coates of the British Trade and Cultural Office, Stephen D. Dunn of the Kaohsiung Branch of American Institute in Taiwan for writing the foreword for this book, my wife with her love, and Kaohsiung Cultural Foundation for sponsoring the publication of this book. Thank you all!

Yu Hsien

September 1, 2000

Kaohsiung, Taiwan

目　錄

序一　*David Coates*
序二　*Stephen D. Dunn*
自序

1. 夫妻樹

水中月（*1974*）…… *2*
盆景的話（*1982*）…… *4*
裸女（*1982*）…… *6*
盆景（*1982*）…… *8*
燭（*1982*）…… *10*
冰心（*1982*）…… *12*
牆（*1982*）…… *14*
吻（*1982*）…… *16*
有了（*1982*）…… *18*
夜（*1983*）…… *20*
中國結（*1983*）…… *22*
剪影（*1983*）…… *24*
疚（*1983*）…… *26*
夫妻樹（*1983*）…… *28*

2. 母親的手

村子裡的路燈（*1984*）…… *32*
魚語（*1984*）…… *34*
壁畫（*1984*）…… *36*
擺渡者（*1984*）…… *38*
六合夜市（*1984*）…… *40*

情婦（ *1984* ）…… *42*
黃道吉日（ *1984* ）…… *44*
石頭記（ *1985* ）…… *46*
那一夜（ *1986* ）…… *48*
母親的手（ *1986* ）…… *50*
舊金山的霧（ *1986* ）…… *52*
看日出（ *1988* ）…… *54*
機上的一夜（ *1988* ）…… *56*
塔的冥想（ *1989* ）…… *58*

3. 影子

靈魂之死（ *1985* ）…… *62*
骨灰罐（ *1989* ）…… *68*
影子（ *1993* ）…… *70*

4. 籠中無鳥

詩與詩人（ *1983* ）…… *74*
悟（ *1984* ）…… *76*
花開的聲音（ *1995* ）…… *78*
殯儀館的化妝師（ *1996* ）…… *80*
詩人和他的情人（ *1996* ）…… *82*
指腹為婚（ *1996* ）…… *84*
蝴蝶蘭（ *1996* ）…… *86*
遊清水寺（ *1996* ）…… *88*

5. 蘋果之傷

京都印象（ *1995* ）…… *92*
長崎蜻蜓（ *1995* ）…… *94*
西湖之晨（ *1996* ）…… *96*

蘋果之傷（*1997*）…………………………………… *98*
雨中蓮（*1997*）…………………………………………… *100*
盜墓（*1997*）……………………………………………… *102*
接生 *DIY*（*1997*）………………………………… *104*
銀婚（*1998*）……………………………………………… *106*

6. 童詩

老榕樹（*1982*）…………………………………………… *110*
奶奶的洗衣板（*1983*）………………………………… *112*
爸爸的鼾聲（*1983*）…………………………………… *114*
看立體電影（*1986*）…………………………………… *116*
音樂枕頭（*1998*）………………………………………… *118*

CONTENTS

Foreword I David Coates
Foreword II Stephen D. Dunn
Preface

I.The Tree Couple

The Moon in Water (1974) 3
Words of a Bonsai (1982) 5
A Nude Maid (1982) 7
The Bonsai (1982) 9
The Candle (1982) 11
The Heart of Ice (1982) 13
The Wall (1982) 15
The Kiss (1982) 17
My Wife Got Something (1982) 19
The Night (1983) 21
A Chinese Knot (1983) 23
The Art of Figure Cutting (1983) 25
Guilt (1983) 27
The Tree Couple (1983) 29

II.Mother's Hands

Streetlights in the Village (1984) 33
Fish Whisper (1984) 35
The Mural (1984) 37
The Ferryman (1984) 39

Liu Ho Night Market (1984) ··································41
Mistress (1984) ··································43
A Lucky Day (1984) ··································45
The Stone (1985) ··································47
On that Night (1986) ··································49
Mother's Hands (1986) ··································51
The Fog in San Francisco Bay (1986) ··································53
Looking at the Sunrise (1988) ··································55
A Night on the Plane (1988) ··································57
The Meditation of the Pagoda (1989) ··································59

III.The Shadow

The Death of Souls (1985) ··································63
The Bone Ash Urn (1989) ··································69
The Shadow (1993) ·································· 71

IV.A Cage of No Bird

Poetry and the Poet (1983) ··································75
Enlightenment (1984) ··································77
The Sound of Blossoming (1995) ··································79
The Cosmetician in the Funeral Parlor (1996) ··································81
The Poet and His Lover (1996) ··································83
A Prenatal Engagement (1996) ··································85
Phalaenopsis (1996) ··································87
Traveling in the Kiyomizudera Temple (1996) ·································· 89

V.The Wound of an Apple

Kyoto Impression (1995) 93
Nagasaki's Dragonfly (1995) 95
The West Lake in the Morning (1996) 97
The Wound of an Apple (1997) 99
A Lotus in the Rain (1997) 101
Tomb Stealing (1997) 103
DIY Delivering (1997) 105
Silver Wedding (1998) 107

VI.Poems for Children

An Aged Banyan Tree (1982) 111
Grandma's Washboard (1983) 113
Daddy's Snore (1983) 115
See a Three-dimensional Movie (1986) 117
The Music Pillow (1998) 119

卷一

夫妻樹

Volume Ⅰ

The Tree Couple

水中月

曾經我的眼
在一面粧鏡前
凝視一朵荷花

而今夕我所見的
是一張蒼白的臉
在變形了的鏡中
扭曲著

這是人間
不是天上

The Moon in Water

In front of a mirror,
My eyes once
Stared at a lotus.

But tonight I see
A pale face
Distorted
By the mirror.

This is the world of mortals,
Not heaven.

盆景的話

小時候
就離鄉背井
來到這有土無地的
院落
仰不見天，俯不及地
總是常被人修剪
且時扭曲成
他們所喜歡的
一種樣子

沒有深植的根
吮水之后
即暗自落淚

故鄉啊
你在哪裏

Words of a Bonsai

Since the childhood
I have been far away from home,
And came to this yard of
Earth but no land.
No sky, no land.
To be always shaped by people,
And twisted into
The style what
They like.

No deep roots,
After drinking the water
I sobbed out lonely tears.

Oh, mother land,
Where are you?

裸女

——題畫

且捨棄虛飾的塵衣
回到初啼那種聖潔
那種真純

讀著妳的冰瑩
讀著妳的嫵媚
讀著妳的豐盈
讀著妳的慵懶

把秀髮讀成垂柳
把眉睫讀成曉月
把眼睛讀成流水
把乳峰讀成山巒
把臀部讀成水彎
把妳讀成荷花
讀成水仙
讀成一面粧鏡
一塵不染

A Nude Maid

—— for painting

Give up that unreal mask,
Come back to the sanctity of the human prime nude
And purity.

Reading your delicacy,
Reading your charm,
Reading your plumpness,
Reading your relaxation.

For long hair read dangling willow,
For eyebrow read dawn moon,
For eyes read brook,
For breast read mountain,
For hip read bay;
Reading you into louts,
Into daffodil
Into a mirror
None dust.

盆景

一輩子
一把泥土就夠了

誰不知
這是一個寸土寸金的世界
祇好將就將就
在這樣一方小屋裡
過它
一輩子

The Bonsai

For a whole life,
A handful of mud is enough.

Everyone knows
This is a world of precious mud.
May not be good enough
In such a small house,
I will live
My whole life.

燭

焚血
煮淚
把黑暗燒出
一個傷口
遁逃

埋首於此，也
焚血，也煮淚， 直至
那一道傷口
縫合

The Candle

Burning the blood,
Cooking the tear,
Burning from the dark
A wound,
Escapes.

I immersed myself in the hard work,
Also burning blood, cooking tear, until
That wound
Has been sewn.

冰心

——獻給李冰老師

所以說
你畢竟是一塊拒絕融化的
冰
以老僧入定的姿態
冷冷地瞪視著
這個變幻無常的
世界

我透視
並且能聽見
那一朵　赤裸的心焰
在你晶瑩剔透的體內
熊熊地
燃燒

The Heart of Ice

—— *dedicated to Ice Lee*

Therefore I thought
You are an ice cube
To refuse melting,
Like an elderly monk concentrated on,
Stared coldly at
The changeable
World.

I look through,
And then heard
The flame of the naked heart
In your crystal body
Burning
Ablaze.

牆

人
走進
一幢最豪華最現代的
老死不相往來的
心房

四周皆牆
牆上都張貼著
保持距離
以策安全

牆裡
牆外
都站著
同樣不得其門而入的
孤寂

The Wall

People
Walk into
A house where heart is
The most luxurious and modern
Never contacted.

The walls all around,
Covered with
"Keep distance
For safety."

Inside,
Outside
Standing
Loneliness
Shut out.

吻

佛曰：不可說，不可說
水仙已吐露著芬芳
闔起你的靈魂之窗吧
讓我溫柔的舟子
與你的舟子會合
且划出我的槳，與你的槳
會師，然後
任湖傾斜，任舟子翻覆

任水淹沒吧
我欲死去
天堂的門已開啟

已微微開啟

The Kiss

The Buddha says, "No words, no words".
The daffodil has sent out the fragrance.
Close your window of the spirit!
Let my tender boat
Meet with your boat;
With our oars intertwining.
The lake on the slant, these two boats are capsized.

Drowned in water!
I am going,
The door of heaven starts to open.

It has slightly opened.

有了

那天
妻對我說 有了
我看了看
我撫了撫
我聽了聽
我笑了笑
什麼也沒說

我想了又想
她是個不懂詩書的
肚裡那來的墨水
那來的真才實學
那來的內在美

有了
終於我對自己說

My Wife Got Something

That day,
My wife told me she got something.
I looked,
I caressed,
I listened,
I smiled,
Said nothing.

I ponder and ponder
She is not educated,
How can she have anything in her brain?
How can she have truly learned?
How can she have inner beauty?

I got it,
At last I talked to myself.

夜

擺脫了戰爭的威脅
遂安全而自由地
回到屬於我倆的
後方

這裏沒有虛偽
沒有噪音
也沒有任何的壓迫感

縱有戰端興起
也只是上帝交下來的
那一回事罷了

雙方無傷亡

The Night

Get rid of the threat of war,
Back to safe and free again
To return to the place that
Belongs to us.

There is no falseness here,
No noise,
Also no pressure.

Even people make war upon nerves,
It would be just an assignment from God,
That's all.

Both of us would be not hurt or die.

中國結

我把心事
編織成一條龍
唱出了
我們
不能再是
一
盤
散
沙

A Chinese Knot

I weave my worries
To be a knot of the dragon.
It sings out --
We can't afford to
Make the knot
Loosen as sand.

Note: Dragon is auspicious creature of China.

剪影

其實
你所看到的
祇是我的一面
另一面
在我心裏

同樣地
我所看到的
也祇是你的一面
另一面
在你心裏

The Art of Figure Cutting

In deed,
What you see
Is my one side only,
The other is
In my heart.

Same goes here
What I see
Is only one side of yours,
The other is
In your heart.

疚

總是五月才想起
在故鄉的妳
想起自己
那些成長的歲月
妳總是以青春的針線
細細地編織著
我們的幸福

總是五月才想起
妳枯樹的容顏
積雪的鬢髮
和空虛的心房

總是五月才想起
妳
是我的
母親

Guilt

Always
Till in May
Am I reminded of
You,
In my hometown
Then I think to myself
Those were the days,
You sew painstakingly your youth into
Our happiness.

Always
Till in May
Am I reminded of
You,
Your Withered face,
Gray hair as snow,
And lonely heart.

Always
Till in May
Am I reminded of
You,
My mother.

夫妻樹

——誌錫婚

我們是
姻緣路上
繾綣纏繞的
雌雄同株

為抓住這方鄉土　這座家園
就這樣同沐陽光和
風雨

青春雖已褪色
容顏卻更耐讀
無論喜悅或憂傷
我們的淚水　總是
如膠似漆

傳說　我們沒有年輪
永恆是年輪
我們沒有名字
名字就叫夫妻

The Tree Couple

—— for tin wedding

We are
On the way, marriage
Twisting with love
On the tree.

To catch our homeland,
Let's live in sunshine,
Wind and rain.

Although our youth has faded,
Our faces are worth reading more.
Whatever pleasure or grief,
Our tears are always
Much more in love.

They says, we don't have any annual cycles,
Eternity is the annual cycle;
We don't have a name,
The name is called a couple.

卷二
母親的手
Volume II
Mother's Hands

村子裡的路燈

從童年的巨木
到如今的金鋼不壞之身
站在路邊
哪有我坐的份

哈！那有什麼關係
這是我的崗位啊
看著夜歸的旅人
我有說不出的喜悅

祇是，我越來越孤寂
孩子們不來玩耍
大人們不來談天
我是越來越孤寂

Streetlights in the Village

The giant wood since my childhood
Became a body of steel,
Standing beside the road
How can I sit upon it!

Ha, it's no big deal,
This is my duty.
To look upon and care for the travelers at night,
I couldn't express how happy I was.

But I was getting lonely and lonely.
Children don't chase here,
And adults don't chat here, neither.
I was getting lonely and lonely.

魚語

那會是
外婆家屋簷下的魚乾串嗎

童年已逝，海已遠
掛在眼前的
是被風過、曝過
僵化了的
自己

忽聞背後
有貓的叫聲傳來

Fish Whisper

Is that fish skewer that
Hanged under my grandmother's eaves?

Childhood has gone, the sea is also far away
Hang in front of my eyes
Blown by wind, dried by sun,
And stiff turned into
Myself.

Suddenly I hear from behind
The sound of a cat coming.

壁畫

在我家書房的牆壁上
有一幅抽象畫
沒有裱褙
也沒有落款
但我知道
那是上帝的傑作
祂用雨水透背
功力十足
就是敦煌的壁畫
也無可比擬

The Mural

An abstract painting
On the wall of my study room.
Not framed,
And no signature found.
I know,
It is God's masterpiece,
He paints on the canvas with rains,
Such craftsmanship can not be compared,
Needless to say of the mural of Tunhwang.

Note: Tunhwang is located in Kansu Province of China. The Caves of
Tunhwang, treasure house of Buddhist scriptures, paintings and statues.

擺渡者

一枝櫓，一張筏
就是你的一生麼

櫓是沒有根的樹
筏是沒有根的萍
你的根在哪裡

渡過了他，又渡過了我
誰來渡你

黃昏了
你的家呢

The Ferryman

An oar, a raft,
Is it your whole life?

An oar is a tree without root.
A raft is a duckweed without root.
Where is yours?

You have ferried him, and me
Who would do this for you?

Sunset is coming,
Where is your ultimate destiny?

六合夜市

你的名字
總在日落后
十分中國的
亮起

亮起一條星河
啊！數不盡的星子
一路游過來
游向不眠的夜裏

好一個雞犬相聞的國度
今夜，就來一道悠然吧
幾碟浪漫，兩杯隨意
並且約好杯底不養金魚

Liu Ho Night Market

Your name,
Very Chinese,
Always brightens up
After the sunset.

Brightens up like a river of stars,
Oh, countless stars,
Swimming along the river,
Swimming through a sleepless night.

How nice to be the neighbor of you!
Tonight, let's enjoy ourselves!
A few dishes of romance, two cups of good moods,
Don't keep golden fish at the bottom of our glass cups.

Note: Liu Ho Night Market is located in Kaohsiung City. "Don't keep golden fish at the bottom of our glass cups." means giving a toast to friends.

情婦

不是水
是比水還要柔的
不是火
是比火還要烈的
不是酒
是比酒還醉人的

我的吉普賽女人啊
水是注定要流浪的
火是注定要燃燒的
酒是注定要醉人的
而妳
注定要成為我心頭的蔦蘿麼

如是
請緊緊地攀爬，緊緊地纏繞
就讓我窒息了吧
我的吉普賽女人啊

Mistress

Not water,
More tender than water.
Not fire,
Hotter than fire.
Not wine,
Drunker than wine.

Oh, my Gypsy woman,
Water is destined to drift,
Fire is destined to be burned,
Wine is destined to inebriate,
And you,
Is destined to be a vine in my heart?

So,
Please climb and twist tightly,
And choke me up.
Oh, my Gypsy woman.

黃道吉日

都選擇這個日子
對面大喜
對面大悲
悲喜之間
僅一條巷道之隔

彼此是鄰居
住在同一條巷道裏
這邊
通向大紅的禮堂
那頭
卻通往黑色的墳場

也是鄰居的我
今天
只好以右臉
陪笑，而以左臉
哭喪

A Lucky Day

Both chose this day,
One side faces exultant,
The other side faces lamenting.
Between exultation and lamentation,
Is only a narrow lane.

They are neighbors,
Living in the same lane.
This side
Leading to a red auditory,
That side
Leading to a black graveyard.

As a neighbor
Today,
My right face
Smiling, but my left face
Crying.

石頭記

沒有佛堂
沒有梵唱
整日我禪坐路旁
如老僧入定

一個醉漢走來
在我身上撒尿
我默默
我只能默默

一個貴婦走來
炫耀我以珠寶
我默默
我還是默默

赤裸如昔
堅硬如昔
我仍是我
一塊石頭

The Stone

No worshipping hall for the Buddha,
No chanting,
All day I sit on the roadside
As an elderly Buddhist monk.

A drunken man approaches
And urinates on me,
I keep silent.
Silent, I am.

A lady approaches
Showing off with jewelry.
I keep silent.
Silent, I am.

Bare as I have been,
Hard as I have been.
Still I am
A stone.

那一夜

——贈韓國女詩人申東春

妳從漢江來
與我的愛河握手
握成什麼呢
姊弟或兄弟都可

在文化中心的晚宴上
妳讀日月潭
我讀妳的眼
妳的眼便美成詩
美成潭，清澈而溫柔

從英雄館到愛河畔
我們共踏輕輕月色
而台灣啤酒
何須邀月成三人

夜已深深
妳北京的夢魘
一再浮現，我不眠的心情

而妳呢
竟以紅腫的眼來回答

On that Night

—— for Tong-choon Shin

You came from the Han River,
Shaking hands with the Love River of mine.
What would it be?
Either brothers or sisters are alright.

At the night party of the Cultural Center,
You read the Sun Moon Lake,
But I read your eyes,
Your eyes beautified as poems,
As the lake, clear and tender.

From the Hero's House to the bank of the Love River,
We walked by moonlight.
To enjoy Taiwan Beer,
We needn't invite the moon to be three's company, need we?

Till a late hour,
Your Peking nightmare
Appeared on my sleepless emotion repeatedly.

And you,
Surprisingly, answered me with the red eyes.

Note:"We needn't invite the moon to be three's company, need we?"
Alludes to a poem by Li Po, a Tan Dynasty poet. "three's company" means the drinker, the moon and the shadow of the drinker.

母親的手

六月，冷冷的回歸線上
陽光攸爾在半空
斷了弦，我們
便進入一個前所未有的
黑暗時代

我來不及抓住
那雙溫暖的手
上帝說，她以散放盡
所有的光與熱
而此刻，我卻無能
回她絲絲的微溫
只能
緊握那雙結繭而冰冷的
手
在世界之外

Mother's Hands

June, the cold tropic,
Sunshine in the sky,
Broke suddenly, we
Got into dark time,
Never happened.

I couldn't catch
The warm hands in time.
God said, she was exhausted
All the light and heat.
But now, I couldn't
Respond her any,
Only can
Hold the cold,
Coarse hands
Beyond the world.

舊金山的霧

或盤桓山頭
或徘徊港灣
或吻住太平洋
或爬上聖瑪琍教堂
或緊跟流浪漢
或尾隨同性戀者
最後，都來到我的稿紙上
成了一首最美麗的
朦朧

The Fog in San Francisco Bay

Lingering on top of the mountain,
Or wandering around the bay,
Or kissing the Pacific,
Or climbing up St. Mary Church,
Or walking after a vagabond,
Or following a homosexual.
At last they all come to my manuscript,
And become the most beautiful
Dimness.

看日出

上山來　這長久的等待
祇為　一瞬間的壯麗

然後　真真知道
花　　是怎樣開放
草　　是怎樣成長
母親　是怎樣用她一生的愛
創造生命的驚喜

Looking at the Sunrise

Coming to the mountain, a long wait,
Only for an instant splendor.

Then we really knew
How flower blooms,
How grass grows,
How the mother creates the blissfulness of life
With love, with her whole life.

機上的一夜

我漸漸遠離我的鄉土
在無垠的夜空

星子，妻不眠的眼
讀著我的飛行

好大的臥房喲
容納了多國籍的夢境

醒來的手，推開日昨的黎明
是太平洋上的一朵奇葩

A Night on the Plane

Far away from my mother land
In the immense night sky.

Stars, my wife's sleepless eyes,
Read my flight.

What a large chamber!
Containing multinational dreams.

Awakening hands push away yesterdawn,
A spectacular flower rises from the Pacific.

塔的冥想

塔裡有人在嗎？

回答我的是
同樣的回聲

祭台上
花兒枯落了
甕罈裡的靈魂們
是否醒著？

正要轉身離去
寺裡的鐘聲，竟無端地
響起

The Meditation of the Pagoda

Anybody in the pagoda?

The answer is
The same echo.

On the altar,
Flowers withered,
Whether the souls in the jar
Are awake?

As I'm turning to leave,
The bell rings in the temple
Without any reasons.

卷三
影子
Volume III
The Shadow

靈魂之死

在異國的夜晚
我孤寂地走著
像荒野的獵人

幾朵廉價的靈魂
開在夜街的角落
沒有燈光，無須月色

一隻耀眼的金絲貓
來到我面前
她以曖昧的眼
向我問路，並且
探測我的體溫
我好奇的心靈

她點燃一根雪茄
又遞給我一支
我沒抽
只探了探她虛掩的胸脯
她問我是不是警察
我搖頭
她還是放心不下
我才堅定地說不

她帶我到一個神秘的海上
歡渡良宵

The Death of Souls

A night in the alien country,
I walked alone
Like a wild hunter.

A few cheap souls
Blossomed on the corner of street,
No light, no necessarity of moonlight.

A charming, golden cat
Came and closed to me.
Her sexual eyes
Asked me the way, and
Touched my temperature,
My curiosity.

She lightened a cigar
And gave me one.
I didn't smoke,
Just looked into her breast with opening careless.
She asked if I was a policeman or not,
I shook head;
She's still worried
So I answered for sure.

She took me to a mysterious ocean
Had a wonderful night.

我們共坐一艘遊艇
好像是粉紅色
她雖看來很年輕
卻像經驗老到的水手
而櫓是她的最初
也是最後的玩具
我乃忘我地划著
逐著金色的水草
駛入幽暗的港灣
時而搖著高大的椰子樹
時而撫摸豐碩的果實
不，這不是椰子樹
椰子樹是不長果實的

風越來越大
浪越來越急
就在這時候
她的船資要求水漲
否則就遭擱淺
祇是
風越來越大
浪越來越急
我怎能就這樣擱淺
好吧
反正我已在鞋內預藏了
歸去的盤纏

We traveled by a boat
Seemed to be a pink one.
She looked very young
But like a well-experienced sailor.
The oar was her first
Also her last toy;
I rowed happily,
Ran after the golden water grass,
Rowed into the dark bay;
Sometimes pushed the coconut tree,
Sometimes caressed the fruits.
No, this isn't a coconut tree
Trees didn't come to fruits.

Getting windy and windy,
Getting rusher and rusher.
At this moment,
She wanted to raise up the fare,
Or stayed traveling.
However
Getting windy and windy,
Getting rusher and rusher.
How could I stop?
Fine!
I'd reserved the money in my shoes
For back home.

喔！茱蒂
妳是我的最初
也是最後的玩具
或許我將再來
但我會牢牢記得
這裡的椰子樹是不長果實的
而我仍是個過客，不是歸人

Oh, Judy
You are my first
Also my last toy.
Maybe I would come back here,
But I would remember
Trees didn't come to fruits,
I'm just a passer-by, not a returnee.

骨灰罐

火化之后
這一塊　一塊
白色的悲傷
一節 一節
黑色的思念
統統放進
這小小　圓圓
冷冷的大理石罐裏
至於
不成塊不成節的
灰
就讓它化作泥
與大地合一

The Bone Ash Urn

After cremation,
Piece by piece
White sorrow,
Piece by piece
Black reminiscence,
All placed into
This little, round
And cool marble urn.
As for remaining
Ashes,
Let them turn into dust
With the earth together.

影子

雲是水的影子
水是雲的影子
詩是畫的影子
畫是詩的影子
你是我的影子
我是你的影子

影子是影子的影子

The Shadow

Cloud is the shadow of water,
Water is the shadow of cloud.
Poetry is the shadow of painting,
Painting is the shadow of poetry.
You are my shadow,
I am yours.

Shadow is the shadow of shadow.

卷四

籠中無鳥

Volume IV

A Cage of No Bird

詩與詩人

1.

如果天空無鳥
如果海洋無魚
如果大地無樹
我不知
那是怎樣的一個世界

如果鳥無天空
如果魚無海洋
如果樹無大地
我不知
那是怎樣的一個世界

2.

為你，我要蓋一棟豪華別墅
為你，我要造一道七彩虹橋
為你，我要做一桌滿漢全席
為你，我要買一件貂皮大衣
而你，你這不識趣的傢伙
竟一一回絶，還説
你所要的，祗是
一間陋室
一條小巷
一道便餐
一襲布衣

Poetry and the Poet

1.
If, no bird in the sky,
No fish in the ocean,
No tree on the earth,
I don't know
What a world it would be!

If, no sky for the bird,
No ocean for the fish,
No earth for the tree,
I don't know
What a world it would be!
2.
For you, I want to build a luxurious villa
For you, I want to make a rainbow-bridge
For you, I want to cook a full formal banquet
For you, I want to buy a mink fur
But you, you don't know anything.
And unexpectedly refuse any offer, and say
What you want, is only
A crude room,
An alley,
A simple meal,
A coarse cloth.

悟

也曾想過　是大鵬
飛越萬水千山
也曾夢過　如白駒
馳騁北國草原
如今啊驚覺
一隻綿羊
在人工的牧場
宿命的生活

而奉獻所有
也祇不過是
那麼一點
皮毛

Enlightenment

I once thought I was a roc,
Which flew over thousand mountains and ten thousand rivers.
I once dreamed to be a white horse,
Rushing over northern prairies.
Oh, now, I am awakened from sleep,
And found that I was a sheep
Living in the artificial ranch,
Predestined.

Only
Fur was
What I could
Contribute.

花開的聲音

—— 給奈由

從神户傳來
花開的聲音
在大阪，深深的夜裡

今年春天
一朵北國的櫻花
去到我遥遠的家鄉
盛放，而就在眼前
她的家鄉
也有醉人的芬芳麼

今夜，在異國的夢土上
會是怎樣美麗而又焦急的
心情，等待著
一朵蓓蕾的
綻放

The Sound of Blossoming

—— for Nayu

The sound of blossoming travels
From Kobe to Osaka
Deep in the night.

This past spring
A sakura from a northern country
Blossomed in my distant homeland
But now
In her homeland
Is there any intoxicating fragrance?

Tonight, in the dream land of an alien country,
How beautiful and unquiet my mind would be,
Awaiting
A bud's
Blooming.

殯儀館的化妝師

許是鬼比人可親
乃選擇面對死亡
面對一成不變的鬼臉
而人是善變的

在陰冷而潮濕的角落
人寐著，鬼醒著
在寐與醒之間
死亡沒有選擇
而天堂和地獄呢
有沒有選擇

其實，鬼和人一樣可憐
面子總是要的
就最後一次吧
讓我好好地玩你
那張不在善變的
臉

The Cosmetician in the Funeral Parlor

Maybe ghost is more friendly than man
So choose to face death,
Face to unchangeable ghostly face,
But man is changeable.

On a could, wet corner
Man sleeping, ghost waking up,
Between sleeping and waking up,
Death has no choice.
But heaven and hell
Do they have any choice?

In fact, ghost is as poor as man.
Face is very important.
This is the last time,
Let me play around with
The unchangeable
Face.

詩人和他的情人

整個上午
詩人和他的情人
在他十八樓的家
讀詩
讀藍藍的天空
有鳥飛過

午后，他們穿越時空
回到遠古
讀陶，情人說
何其年輕，何其年輕哪

然後去西子灣
聽海洋學的課
如聽浪濤
藍藍的天空
有鳥飛過

他們泛著小舟
來到「萊茵河」
這裏距愛河最近
一杯伯爵奶茶
一杯檸檬
竟不覺有一碟蛋糕
一起溶入暮色

註：萊茵河，一家咖啡屋的名字。

The Poet and His Lover

All the morning,
The poet and his lover
In his home on the eighteenth floor,
Reading poems,
Reading the blue sky
The bird flying away.

In the afternoon, they flew over time and space
And returned to ancient time
Reading pottery, his lover said,
"How young we are!"

They went to the His-tzu Bay then
Listen to the oceanography
Listen billow,
In the blue sky
The bird flew away.

They went boating
And came to the "Rhine",
Here was the nearest to the Love River.
A cup of Earl Grey with milk,
A glass of lemonade,
Unexpectedly there was a dish of cake
Dissolving into sunset.

Note: Rhine is a coffee shop.

指腹為婚

——給美雲

聽說在我未出世以前
有一朵雲
在未醒來的天空
等待今世的姻緣

天空醒來
雲醒來
妳我錯身而過
愛在銀河擱淺

而來世呢？妳來不來
誰知道
妳是天上飄忽的雲
還是地上流動的水

A Prenatal Engagement

—— *for Mei-win*

They said before I was born
There's a cloud,
The sky hasn't woken yet,
Looking forward to marrying this life.

The sky woke up
And so did the cloud.
You and I blunder away each other,
Our love got stranded in the Milky Way.

But how is the future? Do you come?
Who did know?
Were you a vagrant cloud
Or a flowing water?

蝴蝶蘭

如果你是一隻蝶
我是什麼呢
今夜，莊周來不來

如果你是一朵花
我是什麼呢？
明早，蘭兒開不開

如果，蝶非蝶，花也非花
妳是什麼呢

Phalaenopsis

If you were a butterfly,
What were I ?
Tonight, would Chuang-tzu come?

If you were a flower,
What were I?
Tomorrow morning, would the flower blossom?

If the butterfly were not butterfly; flower, either,
What were you?

遊清水寺

且讓我進入你的透明裏

來，取一瓢水
一瓢清清的水
心便充滿法喜

啊十一面觀音
看你千手千眼，看你
入定青山，鳥瞰紅塵
多少朝代更迭，繁華落盡
而山仍是山，你仍是你

聽説，春天的櫻花
秋天的楓葉，最美
祈求愛情婚姻
健康財富，都靈
啊十一面觀音，其實
我只在乎你，在乎你
取一瓢水，
一瓢清清的水

Traveling in the Kiyomizudera Temple

Let me come into your delicacy!

Come, fetch a ladle of water,
A ladle of limpid water,
My heart, full of pleasure.

Oh, Guanyin of eleven faces,
Gaze at your thousand hands and thousand eyes, gaze and gaze
The mountain, the mundane world.
Though many dynasties founded and overthrew, blossom flowers fell down,
But mountains are still mountains, you are still you are.

They said, sakuras in the spring
Maples in the autumn are the most beautiful
Pray for love and ideal marriage,
Pray for health and wealth, all come true.
Oh, Guanyin, eleven faces,
In fact, I only care about you , care about you,
Fetch a ladle of water,
A ladle of limpid water.

Note:Buddhist bodhisattva of fertility.

卷五
蘋果之傷
Volume V
The Wound of an Apple

京都印象

街道，很長安

遲暮美人走來
歌舞伎走來
老和尚也從唐朝走來
敲響古剎的鐘聲
鴿子們依然入定
老和尚說：喫茶去
而我的銀碗盛雪
老和尚揮了揮毫
那蒼勁的筆法
力透紙背，可讀出
中國的歷史

而奶奶咳嗽不止
御苑寂寂

Kyoto Impression

Street, like Chian-an.

An old beauty comes here,
Geishas come here,
The old monks come here from Tang Dynasty, too,
And knock the bell in the old temple.
The doves deep into meditation.
An old monk says that let's have tea,
But my silver bowl fills with snow.
The old monk waves the brush pen,
What a strong stroke
We could read
Chinese history.

But my grandma still coughs,
And the Imperial Garden keeps silence.

長崎蜻蜓

早上，我的右腳
剛剛抽離廣島
下午，我的左腳卻又跌入
長崎的深淵

戰爭坐此哭誰
半個世紀了
鴿子依然紅著眼
咕咕唱著
和平，和平

一隻蜻蜓飛來
我神經質地舉起攝影機
將之
擊落

Nagasaki's Dragonfly

In the morning, my right foot
Just left Hirosima;
In the afternoon, my left foot fell in
Nagasaki's abyss.

Wars sat here crying for whom?
Half century has passed
Doves still had tears in their eyes,
Cooing for
Peace, peace.

A dragonfly came flying.
I raised a camera sensitively,
Shoot it
Down.

西湖之晨

潑墨
七月的江南
慢，慢
暈染開來

遠山，近水
我在其中

西子醒來，東坡醒來
從古老的詩句裏
悠悠醒來

而半寐半醒的我
卻一腳跌入
深深的
鄉愁

The West Lake in the Morning

Landscape painting with a splash,
Chiang-nan in July,
Slowly, slowly,
Dyeing.

Far mountain, near water,
I'm among them.

Hsi-tzu wakes up, Dong-po wakes up
From classic verse,
Wake up slowly.

But I'm half in sleeping,
And I fall into
A deep, deep
Nostalgia.

蘋果之傷

穿著紅衣裳的蘋果們
在水果店裡
展示美的存在
期待有人來愛

我挑了其中一個
她的姿色迷人
且散發誘人體香
我褪去她的衣裳
卻見遍體鱗傷

我左思右想
終於褪去自己的衣裳
看自己的胴體
不也遍體鱗傷

赤裸裸的我
握著赤裸裸的蘋果
仔細端詳，且輕輕剜去
她的憂傷

The Wound of an Apple

Apples wearing red clothes,
In the fruit shop
Showing the existence of beauty,
Expecting somebody to love.

I chose one of them,
She was very charming,
And emitted perfume from her body.
I took off her clothes,
Many wounds all over her body.

I thought over and over,
Finally I took off my own clothes.
And looked at my own body,
I was not free from wounds myself.

As nude as I was,
Held the nude apple,
I stared carefully, and picked out
Her grief lightly.

雨中蓮

五百年前，妳我的相遇
在一個夏日的黃昏
寂靜的小鎮上
雨，梵唱著
空靈而淒美，妳的容顏
慈悲而聖潔
蓮藕在泥中修行
妳在人間，纖纖不染
若我是蓮，必心心相印
若我是蛙，是蜻蜓
必伴每一朵蓮
守著風雨，守著妳
五百年後，若有來生
換我是妳，妳是我
當更能體會
我對妳的愛有多美，多苦
如那容顏，如那蓮心

A Lotus in the Rain

Five hundred years ago, our encounter
In a summer dusk,
A small and silent town.
Rain singing lightly,
Easy and sad, your face
Mercy and sanctification.
Lotus roots practice Buddhist in the mud,
You are in the world with pureness.
If I were a lotus, be love each other
If I were a frog, a dragonfly
Companion with every lotus
Keep wind and rain, keep you.
Five hundred years later, if we had next life
Let's change the role each other,
You must know how much I love you
How beauty the lotus face is,
How bitter the lotus heart is.

盜墓

佛說：我不入地獄，誰入地獄
況這世界太小
去向地獄移民或許
也是不錯的
一種方式

然則，今晚去探個路吧
好圓個淘金夢
讓今聲痛痛快快
來世誰理它呢

而今夜，越黑風高
神不之鬼不覺的
只是，沒想到
迎面而來的竟是
祖爺爺烈齒狂笑的
兩排
假牙

Tomb Stealing

Buddha says, "If I don't get into the hell, who does?"
This is a small world,
Immigrate to the hell maybe
A good idea.

So, let's explore tonight
For fulfilling the money dream.
Be happy in this life.
Who cares in next life?

Tonight, no moon and no wind,
Neither God nor ghost knows anything.
But they really don't think that
They see
Grand-grandfather laughs with ripping mouth,
And shows his two rows of
Dentures.

接生 DIY

那天清晨，她把浴室當產房
把馬桶當床
以她的纖纖小手，接生自己

一切來得突然
來不及陣痛就醫
來不及向老公嬌嗔
好好啃他的骨咬他的肉
頑皮的小生命就急急來到這世界

從浴間傳來美麗的初啼
驚醒沉睡中的父親
啊我兒，你卻這般迫不及待
與我見面

胎盤和臍帶一起脫落
孩子，你要學會獨立
這是一個自助的年代
就像母親，在馬桶上
自助，生下了你

DIY Delivering

In that morning, she made bathroom as delivery room,
Had toilet as bed,
Delivered herself with her little hands.

Everything came suddenly
She didn't feel pain and see a doctor yet,
Didn't make a feminine anger to her husband,
And chewed his bone and bit his flesh,
A naughty small life came to this world urgently.

Beautiful and primary crying came from the bathroom
Waked his father up from deep sleep.
Oh, my son, you were so hurry
To see me.

Placenta and navel string dropped down together.
My son, you have to learn how to be independent,
This is a DIY generation.
As your mother, sat on the flush toilet,
DIY, delivered of you.

銀婚

那年妳廿三，我廿四
牽手清冷的禮堂
公證人一聲相愛嗎，印證
我們堅定的愛情

四分之一世紀是漫長還是一晃
血流過，汗淌過
上山下海過
哭過、笑過、鬧過
酸甜苦辣過
一部滄桑史就寫在臉上
寫在心中

而今年，老大廿四，老么廿三
我變老了，妳也是
牽起妳結繭的手
什麼都不必說，我知道
妳願意繼續走下去
直到地老
天荒

Silver Wedding

That year you were twenty-three, I was twenty-four,
Hand in hand in the cold auditory,
Notary asked if we loved each other, proving
Our stony love.

A quarter of century, long or short?
Blood flowed and sweat dripped,
Up and down to the mountain and sea,
Crying, laughing , playing what we had,
Tasted the lives of sour, sweet, hard, hot.
History was written on our face,
Impressed in our heart.

Now, our old child twenty-four, young-one twenty-three,
I am getting older and you, too.
Hand your coarse hands,
You don't have to say anything, I know,
You love to go ahead with me.
To outlast even the heaven
And the earth.

卷六
童詩
Volume VI
Poems for Children

老榕樹

樹公公真逗趣
他有好多好長的翫鬚
不是黑也不是白
他最喜歡風奶奶
只要她一來
他便忘我地盪著鞦韆
風奶奶走了
樹公公又回到了往日的寂寞

An Aged Banyan Tree

A funny tree-grandpa,
He has many long beards,
Neither black nor white.
He likes wind-grandma very much.
When grandma comes
He's swinging, forgets who he is.
When she is gone
Tree-grandpa comes back to the loneliness of his old days.

奶奶的洗衣板

奶奶的洗衣板
向她自己的臉
歷盡滄桑的樣子
祇是我不懂
為什麼板上的皺紋
愈來愈模糊
而奶奶臉上的皺紋
卻愈來愈深

Grandma's Washboard

Grandma's washboard
Like her wrinkly face,
Experienced the days.
I really don't understand
Why the washboard's wrinkle
Getting vaguer and vaguer,
But grandma's wrinkle
Getting deeper and deeper.

爸爸的鼾聲

爸爸的鼾聲
像山上的小火車
使我想起美麗的森林

爸爸的鼾聲
總是斷斷續續的
我真擔心火車滑下來

咦！爸爸的鼾聲停了
是不是火車到站了

Daddy's Snore

Daddy's snore
Like the small train on the mountain,
Make me remind of the beautiful forest.

Daddy's snore
Always fitful,
I do worry that the train will slip down.

Yi, Daddy's snore stops,
Does the train get into the station?

看立體電影

蝶兒飛過來，飛過來了
我伸手一捉
捉了個空

魚兒游過來，游過來了
我伸手一抓
抓了個空

哎呀！不得了
這回老虎撲過來了
快逃命呀

See a Three-dimensional Movie

Butterflies are flying toward me,
I catch them at once,
But nothing.

Fish are swimming toward me,
I catch them at once,
But nothing.

Ay, it's too bad,
A tiger makes a pounce upon me,
Let's run away quickly!

音樂枕頭

我有兩個枕頭
一個布做的
一個爸爸的肚子
有時，我和爸爸玩累了
就枕在他的肚子上
軟軟的，很有彈性
還可以聽到美妙的音樂
聽著聽著就睡著了

The Music Pillow

I have two pillows.
One is made of cloth,
The other is daddy's tummy.
Sometimes I play tired with daddy,
And pillow on his tummy,
Feel soft and elastic.
I can hear sweet music,
Listen and get to sleep.

國家圖書館出版品預行編目資料

機上的一夜 / 雨弦著 .-- 初版 .-- 臺北市：
文史哲，民 90
面； 公分
中英對照
ISBN 957-549-344-3(平裝)

1.

851.486 90000576

機上的一夜

著　　　者：雨　　　　　　　　　　　弦
出　版　者：文　史　哲　出　版　社
登記證字號：行政院新聞局版臺業字五三三七號
發　行　人：彭　　　　正　　　　雄
發　行　所：文　史　哲　出　版　社
台北市羅斯福路一段七十二巷四號
郵政劃撥帳號：一六一八〇一七五
電話 886-2-23511028. 傳眞 886-2-23965656
封面設計：張　　　　秀　　　　蘭
印　刷　者：功　名　印　刷　公　司

實價新臺幣一六〇元

中華民國九十年一月初版

ISBN 957-549-344-3